soft urgency

soft urgency

poems   megan leick

for Raelia Rose Pennenberg,
and the inexplicable impact her life and death imparted
on me. and for those who feel that they have nothing
left, a reminder: you can still write.

contents

summer

ripping open each other's chests:
do you like the view?
disclosure reciprocity
bruising our tender skin
like a fruit

trading hats
bargaining warmth
bodies that seem to rhyme

blackberry brandy
and fire tongues /
following the pennies
that led me to your side

// becoming familiar //

the reflection of fingertips
playing shadow puppets
(youthful guise)
on the soft light
bouncing off her back /
a reflexive arch
a ripple of sweet warmth and buzz
to what might come next

// foreshadow //

i'm in the place i have
been to the most /
but with you here
it's a shade more yellow /
a size larger /
trees stand on their heads
for fun
and animals slink near
our side:
anomalous
alive /
not a change of scenery
but fresh eyes to see it with

i could get used to this
rosy retina life

// you open my eyes //

i picture our bodies
our hands
our mouths
drowning in each other on an unmade bed /
in the pressing darkness
with alcohol
burning our lungs

but i also see us on a
sunday morning /
with the light
and books
and coffee
and our eyes
saying everything and nothing
all
at
once

// i want all of it //

the melodies from the night train stumbled over and over themselves—creating a cacophony of sounds.

but none like the frequency of your prosody, giving life to strings of words, collecting around my ear, being hungrily consumed by my brain.

the earth quakes, yet we sit heavy—gravity originating from the spot where the center of my spine rounds into the front of your chest, pulling through jackets and bone.

you label train cars, describe what materials they haul, which were best for riding in and why—reminding me that there was a story about you i have not yet fully read.

....

that night, you told me how your heart felt—before and after the in-between, when the train pushed across the landscape—your words resonating across me like a bell, but i can still feel them now, a soft sweet ripple out from the middle of my spine.

something changed when you entered the scene. i should have guessed as much, you with adventure and home stained all over your hands.

// the night we found a spot to watch the trains and you told me how your heart felt //

take my afflicted edges
keep throwing me back /
let those soft summer tides
work on my skin

the water reminds me of the way
she holds my hand /
washing me back
to her shores
pulling me in stronger
every time she
beckons me to come near

salt and dirt and scales
slip around these opaque edges /
who echo stories
from when they were chipped and
scratched up
by those with weapons under
coats and on tongues

but here, with her
i am reminded of my softness /
of the thick emotion
layered throughout

throw me back to the waves:
see how gentle i can become

// sea glass //

thoughts of you during the day /
i roll them around in my mouth
careful not to linger
on any memory too long /
like hard candies
i hesitate
to make these memories
last /
if i'm patient
i may spend every moment
this way /
until i'm not caught in the crossfire
of holding onto memories
and i can hold you

// daydreaming //

she's waxing and waning
would you look at her sky
so far away
so high, so high
so way out there
they reach with their lines /
formulate wishes
craters under her eyes /
a pale pretty dip in her back
the fading whisper of a smile
reveals her compassion: luminous, wide

// contemplations on moon phases //

i found you sitting on the
concrete step
outside my door like the
sunday morning comics

// come inside //

the lens between our gaze /
your cracked, careful hands and
camera covering all but the
smile's wrinkle lines:
squirming in my seat /
i start to blush as you still the frame
looking down like i'm shy
bumping into you with my eyes

snap me out of this frozen moment
and make me white /
steal glances at what's developing
a link to this night

// polaroid memories //

pollinate me
summer baby
made of heavy heat /
satin sheets
dew-holding leaves

walk me through your garden
leave with a tongue
stained green /
tuck flowers:
spaces in-between
and unseen

river eyes
flood my mind /
clothes on
i dive

// blooming next to you //

we lie right where we need to be on sunday mornings:
your lips in my hair
your lips across my shoulder
your lips on my lips
the quilt shoved off the bottom of our
mattress in the corner of that crumbling room
       the curtains with their frayed edges half open
       sneaking in the sun that aches of summertime
       at full—unabashedly full—brightness
the coffee, grown cold in our lazy forgetfulness
       made much too bitter for my liking
       and much too sweet for yours
my bangs tickle my lashes
       and the scruff on your cheeks tickle everything else
the neighbor dogs bark
the rattling of the heater
the dripping of the swollen ceiling
       we don't hear any of it
thoughts of the past softly
shift like clouds near our heads
       the way you found me
       on the 17th of august
       with a ringing in my ears
       and cracks on my lips
i rest a sun-kissed cheek on your arm
       with the scar that you will never tell me about
and we settle right back where we need to be
on sunday mornings

// i'll find you when i need you //

pressing your fragrant flora
—holding fast—
patient to your petals whose fumes my tongue
caress /
pray: dry dry dry but do not crack

moon watches with care
—mood light, big solitary balloon—
at a woman with a wide pumpkin smile:
spinning
stitching in circles
slipping in cracking alien mud
just to reach
hands like a child, fuss and cry
to press her prettier
satin foraged sweetie /
bruising praying knees: stay stay stay

// i never felt this way before //

fall

i am dying

i have known for years:
first came the dread, a heavy quilt
over my head in the evening /
and the mold, i smelt it on my breath
brushed my teeth until the gums bled /
i lost weight, my bones sharp and hollow
shivers in the summertime and
hungry for sweaters /
i gave away the clutter and my time
to the people i missed when they were
in the other room /
and drank words from their hands until
my stomach bloated because the fear
held its tongue in the
presence of their wisdom /
i made love to the idea of immortality
but he didn't see forever in me /
and i walked through thorns to
punish my skin, decided to
shun the home i crouched in

i am alive for now and so are you /
but i regret to inform you
you are dying too

// livingdying //

we wanted the future in our hands:
to knead / pinch / and cut into
desirable shapes

it was youth and naivety and
now i see
that no matter the
shapes we created
it was going to happen
exactly as it was suppose to /
and the storyline between us
would end too soon

// premature endings //

remember arivaca / with her dried up creeks and dried up plants and dried up air / with the bluestem prickly poppy in unison pulling me close to glimpse the softness of her petals and keeping me away with her crown of thorns, teaching me an important lesson about this place where i'm a visitor.

remember arivaca / where baboquivari peak watched over us, guarding this place and her people / our eyes continuously finding her to guide our way, same as the desert crossers before and after us.

remember arivaca / when we crawled on hands and knees up crumbling trails, bulging packs filled with small comforts gathered for the travelers / fiber one brownie bars, cans of vienna sausages, gallon jugs of water, socks.

remember arivaca / where the sound of a million bees buzzing slammed into our eardrums and our amygdala's for minutes, and then hours, as a border patrol helicopter (filled with the kind of people who orchestrate other people's deaths) circled us as we hiked.

remember arivaca / where my steps were stiff with the fear of stumbling across death on our path / with the fear of a low-flying helicopter that would force the scattering of us, or of the desert crossers later that night / with the fear of the supplies we so carefully delivered to the desert being slashed and destroyed

by the border patrol before it could make it to the
hands of people who are at the hands of fate.

i remember because i can not forget the controversy
/ the greed and filth, the strength and hope / and
because i still hear that helicopter circling us all, in
disguise as safety, but with the name of violence.

// the protectors, the destroyers //

a front row seat
VIP experience /
what a view:
big-bold fake-gold
arches / crosses / alter
polished wooden pew; i slip and slide /
naked earth-quaking legs
sprouting from a floral dress
("i do not want to wear black") /
sanguine hands being bitten bloody
like i've been fighting battles all week
          which i have
until it's my turn to stand, walk
grab the handles of the
heavy wooden box /
i don't even try to remain composed:
grief is explosive

// funeral //

she wants to be examined
studied
and defined /
but not with labels, statistical figures

she wants to be contemplated
            as students in an art museum gaze
hushed
admiring form
            and shape
                        and color
in the unassuming, full light

she wants to be unclothed
            and real /
in her nakedness, they will feel
threads
aching to be pulled
to sing the story of her body and of
the soft creature nesting inside

she wants to be pale and freckled and curved
            the external so visceral you
are holding without
holding /
and for the inner art
to be perceived by dwelling on the
            gentle spot inside her upper arm
            the space around her hip bone
            and the skin around her thumbs

she wants to be
she wants to be
i want to be

// but why does it feel inconceivable to be
yourself and be loved at the same time //

today is the day
the big weigh-in /
a courtroom tragedy
coming to a full boil
the tension about to pop the lid /
your feet spaced equally apart
stand straight and let them Calculate
Debate /
hands clenched at the sides
you look straight ahead
because of bravery or pain /
but my eyes are down down
down 10 feet underground /
where it does not seem to
fucking matter
the number of years /
nothing will bring her back to life

the sentence echoes around the room /
finding us both
in the corner of the eye

// the verdict //

the sky is an artist /
she paints
when she can't cage up
the trojans
in their wooden horses
anymore /
using her paintbrush:
the rain.
the water makes
her world
a shade darker /
the grass
a nourished green /
the rocks
a hallowing gray /
the river
a churning brown.
it even paints me /
that's why i relish
it so much /
it makes me
another color
so that others
don't recognize me
under raindrop hair
and slippery skin /
(slick in order
to make the
great escape).
sometimes /
the rain changes me

so much that i can
climb out
of my body's cocoon /
and see myself
from the outside.
i wonder what
kind of person
i've become /
i wonder how long
i've been falling
until i realized i
fell.

// have i always been breaking or did that day
break me //

she repeats their names in her head
like a thousand year old chant /
becoming more raw as she feels the weight

she breaths their syllables out:
they form ephemeral clouds
in the cold that bloodies her throat

she sucks in meretricious cigarettes
bought with a few dollars and the
coins she peeled off the icy ground

she drums her foot nervously, why?
(the buzz in her bloodstream?)
(the temperature stealing time?)

no

the disturbed dirt /
grass roots grasping hold /
rocks, worms, readjusting to accommodate
two wooden boxes
interrupting the fluency
contained underneath the chaos above

no

she stands transfixed
as if her body was being paralyzed from the inside /
the only sign, her pleading eyes
she mumbles the prayers from her childhood
(foreign as they rush out from corrupted lips) /

possessed by a need to believe in something, anything

no

this is not the girl who has it all:
this is the girl who falls apart in the sticky dark
and waits indefinitely for someone to turn on the light

// standing by their graves //

on the day i am to die
i will know by the
      heavy desire
to scoop handfuls of dirt
the people stomp over
      and swallow it

i have taken from earth
all my life:
when will she take me back
      recycle me

// from dust to dust //

someone has been
breaking into my mind
hijacking the memories
taking her from
mine

felt like a hammer to my cortex
when her memory lost
          shape - smell - movement - time
not yet ready to submit
to synaptic pruning of unspoken lines
i keep an investigation board
tracking liquid details
and pinning them down /
together, there is life
in the way they rhyme:
          videos - perfume - photos - letters - stories
climbing mountains just to ask
about her to the sky
tying a rock to my ankle
and sinking
to comprehend what it is to die

you see
i know she exists around me
i'm just too human to say "hi"
physically chained to this dimension
a slave to the pennies i beg
she dropped on the supermarket floor
for me to find

// you live in my mind //

missing time /
dry mouth out of rhymes
letters left unsent—yellowed by light /
soft and sweet as cattail shells unfolding
take me slowly—take my life /
eyes spread wide, I'll walk until i find:
healing in the hollows that i've writhed

plant my head under snow in wintertime /
will i bloom or mold through the fight?
i move away in slow motion
detox from your mind:
the hawks are circling, leave me one more time

hesitate
before the sharp break
when the branch shudders under our weight /
let's leave slow, like day to night
with peace with fading of light /
i hope to see you again
and if i don't, i'll remember when

// slow goodbye //

you have been dead 5 years
"i can't believe it's been that long"—they say
      i can
my past and future, the mundane everyday
have been diffused of you by time /
like droplets falling on
the watercolor painting of your portrait /
like the foreboding grains of sand in an hourglass
reminding me that synaptic connections die

used to pick the scab over memories of you
to make it bleed
to see you in my minds eye as you used to be
but those in the land of the living
advised against it
      and i let the scab become a scar

i see its controversy
to the cyclic way of life
yet
i miss the open wound
a way for me to hold your death and life
in a way i could control
in a way so vivid

i can't find enough
color in this place to paint you anew
from the image in my dulled memory

// to move on / to hold on //

the day pain chooses you
it will be clear /
she does not follow a schedule
nor give a warning /
she shows up at your house
and without a knock
barrels in with luggage under her arms
she unpacks on the floor in your room /
how long will she stay?
it could be a night
or nights /
not even she knows
driven by the unpredictability
of the next moment, the next bruised fate /
she is a burden /
she will draw emotions out of you
that you did not know you contained /
and when she is gone
you will promise to yourself she will
never
come back /
but she will /
and so you take it all again

// we are built to feel pain; so feel it //

winter

a pair of peppermint lungs
cracked open—crackling /
flames taking it out on
obituaries
advertisements
testimonies /
unbutton that jacket of ribs
pull   apart   muscles
            reverse to their purpose
of existing to keep the bones from
bursting open /
expose the lungs shivering
beneath

bribe the body
to lay down
(in a parasympathetic way)
in front of the flames /
to unpack
bags inside
bags under eyes /
looking unfamiliar
and painfully the same /
blue
     bluer
          bluest
what has the cold done with the people?

// it's not the thing that will kill me; it's the
aftermath //

the poetry found, then
stalked me /
lingered like cigarettes on fingertips and
catcalled me

she stroked my cheek, then
slapped me /
held me under in the bathtub, then
revived me

lifted her skirt up her thigh, she
seduced me /
then made me kiss the concrete

she put words one-by-one
on the tip of my tongue
like water to the dehydrated /
but i was drowning

it's a chase dynamic
the definition of addiction /
the way i beg to her verses
to save my corpse in an IV

// terms and conditions //

when i was 14, a tornado slung its heavy
arm across my parent's property /
heard no siren in our deep sleep /
after, we crept out of the house to breath
in the aftermath:
words and belongings hanging from trees
and ripped into pieces

....

when she met him, there was no weather warning
and she was asleep to signs of the mysterious calm developing /
his persistent, building force entered the scene yet
she neglected to notice the similarities

he assured, i don't break people, i break things
as if it was any consolation /
smashed fence panels
shattered mixtape cd
wrecked car
cracked glasses
torn skin on his arm

he was a tornado
billowing over top everything she could see /
until there was just her and him
battling with the doorknob of her bedroom
at the moment she realized, she was a thing

// before they bite, they bark //

peeking through the spaces in the blinds at the cold air
fingers, wrists, covered with mango juice, absently sticky
stale cereal on a sunday morning and spoiled milk
half-finished letters spread like a tablecloth
spaghetti stains on a shirt from last week
dusty car sinking into the concrete

// quarantined in a pandemic //

tar bubbles from the blacktop
sizing up worn-down soles
sticking and slurping
bus stop blues
lips
blowing cigarette
smoke (he probably needs)
eyes to the floor
to the floor
the floor
floor of the bus
blown up knuckles
have a stern talk with the seat
during bumps and
turns and
stops
step off
step careful
set time aside to
suspiciously elude
cracks in the concrete
dirty weeds dominating there
POP
monday's
sale beer, a cough
grey bubbles settle
in their host: seven more
seven thousand more
bubbles
dirtied
fingernails

drag jerky and blind
down the dim-lit hallway
delivering him to
a bed

// a man in the city //

i will take the blame
and i'll take it again
and i'll take it again
if you ask with enough fire from your
lungs/tongue /
because i don't mind
adding scrap wood
to the fire
i keep burning in honor
of the darkest parts of me

this fire is a monster /
always hungry
always inspecting:
        length of my stride
        cracks in my lips
        volume of my laugh
        size of my pants
        color of my underwear

i do not mind being the loser of this story /
realized that sometimes
that is exactly what those who
claimed to love me, wanted me to be /
i did not start this fire
but i can't let it die
(i can't remember what it feels like
to not be burning alive.)

// blame game //

stairway scramble
a fumble of arms
vocalize
terror–eyes
blank / alcohol gaze
and a frog pinned down
to experiment, to play /
the paint drips down the walls
and drawls:
"you were asking for it"
"he's not the type" /
then a moment
a breakaway;
the bird flies—
face stiff with
salivation
from the bear inside—
only to bully herself after
"get your shit together!"
removing his spit in the
community bathroom /
the washcloth rubbed so hard
it could have been sandpaper
for the way it left rashes on her
cheeks

// he was a friend //

the plane window plays mediator
between my forehead and the air outside:
i fantasize the drama of a pinprick hole
interrupting the division /
the angry suck of air through diffusion
and from my lips and skin

will the pressure chew on me
spit me out
—a cherry pit—
into my hungry fate beneath

// feeling empty on a plane ride from alaska
at 2 am; i didn't sleep the whole night //

you told me you put work into me /

i never felt you work for me
the only thing i saw you work on was a memory /
wrote more poems about me than you could've with sanity
when i said goodbye /
put me through a machine
wringing me out until i was not me /
every part of me tainted as cruel
as mean /
i lived rent free
in your vindictive imagery

it happened in the leaving /
you couldn't believe
that a girl who couldn't love herself
was capable of separating two beings /
you held me under a microscope tainted with
a bloated sense of self
writing a letter detailing—chronologically—
my faults as a human being /
(i still have not forgiven you for those words)

felt your hand around my neck until it wasn't me
because you're destructive /
narcissism will do that /
it doesn't see reality
it only sees something like cruelty
that you believe you have the personal privilege
to know the feeling of /
you claimed injustice and abandonment

while i was busy setting myself free from manipulation /
and a relationship that was always being
worked on
but never working

// revenge //

unstick eyes:
morninglight
blinds /
snap on a set of
crackling lungs and
shrug off the mascara
forgotten last night /
spirit hanging at half-mast
"extra coffee?"
"i'm fine" /
line up the
remedies and bottles:
shake - pop - bye? /
pack:
        food
        thick, old books
        some kind of smile

"excuse me,
is it warmer here?"

// winter women //

boughs hanging heavy
      where the f- is spring?
fingers cross inside mittens
eyelash ink paints skin
circadian rhythm on spin cycle
quilts on blankets on a
short of breath
human being

// dreams of some(place)(thing)(body) warmer //

he said we were waiting for a sign /
kept checking the sky
like a kid looking for airplanes /
it might come today:
the slender bodies of the sandhill cranes
and the release of sap from maple trees

he kept quieting me to check the
sound waves (we might
hear them before we see them) /
and in the meantime
steady work
drilling the trees
(drops of watery sap falling
onto my finger
        and i eagerly lick them clean)

and then, with a noiseless crash:
the next hole i drill spills
the tree's sap down her trunk /
the crane call quietly reverberates
against the trees /
i exclaim /
he hushes me /

. . . .

i want order
like sandhill cranes returning home
and sap spilling from trees
        synchrony and sense and reassurance /
i want signs
and all i get is chaos

violence
brain explosions
eyes wide awake in the night
staring at the ceiling
and not thinking
but not sleeping /
it feels like
      half eaten candies, stuck
      to the wrapper /
      the flame in the woodstove
      repeatedly withering out /
      coffee stains on a book
      obscuring the ending /
      the voice of a lover 2,430
      miles away /
      missed train connections /
      half-finished thoughts that

// maybe one day it will all make sense //

as spring serves herself to earth's plate /
wet and heavy crystals
cling, then slip:
i melt them/you
the thump of snow slipping from branches
befalling my shadow
as i go go go
as quick and damp as rage and
as the hand you clench /

i don't know now and i didn't then
why the leaving was stuck
        fat globus sensation in my throat
guess my fingers were frozen around your name / like a
tongue to a flagpole
we were more than an unfortunate match
        you were a trap

// spring cleaning myself of you //

spring

the slow coming spring thaw
lays its palms on the head of the
shudder-quiet mountain valley

she holds snow to her chin
as a white quilt
reluctant to shed a layer

sounds of a crystal chandelier
born from the trickle of the
cool runoff
and tempting to fingertips that
give way to goosebumps

// as she thaws, i mirror her movements //

it is time

time for you to take out
those clothes
you have washed
so
many times
the colors have
faded   blended   grayed
they have waited for you
gave you space
going around and around just like
the spinning
in your head

but it is time to
hang them on the line
and then
dress yourself in them
(they are   empty
of all the memories that
stained them)

gentle soul
you have been
a b s o l v e d

// the compass is pointing toward yourself //

air
handed to me on a platter /
an all you can eat event

i'm greedy /
hands spreading
mouth open /
storing it like an animal

it is more than i can perceive:
the oxygen
hanging fat, like
apples from the trees /
in this place

// the air is different here; i can breath //

i make preparations to transplant my smell
belongings, fingerprints
to another space /
shoulder blades (as heels
digging into the dirt)
crawl around the backs of chairs and hold on /
the feeling of home caffeinates me;
it is my ritual, my comfort /
a point of conviction amongst uncertainty

yet material items have been boxed up and I tread
from room to bare room
packing away the attributes
in attempts to take all that i can
in my car and in my mind:
cataloging the color of the walls
and the dips in the floorboards
backing out of the house and going back in
just to remember how it smells
stepping on the squeaky spots in the stairs
and pulling my sweater around me tighter
as i glance at the wood stove clicking with heat /
not looking back
as i step out the door

and into my innominate room:
colors, smells, imperfections
all dusty and unnamed /
i push boxes around and
familiarize, acclimate, adapt /
i find the light switches and

hammer nails into the wall, steam up the
bathroom when i shower, smoke weed in bed
and put the needle on a record

and i fall in love again with a rented room
because it is where i am
and where i must bloom or mold /
it is where my sound and light
reflects, where the clothes i wear
and the books i read and the art i made
reside. because it is what i have chosen it to be
and where i have let the vulnerable threads of the
soft creature of my body
unwind and breathe /
it is temporary - but it is home;
and that is enough

// moving day //

for a moment /
i let myself become
so stagnant
stiff
and old-leather tough

where did the dare in my eyes
go?

it is time to bring her back:
born so soft
but rimmed with fire /
i forgot i was both

// becoming brave //

she used to melt like candle-wax /
she would enter the room, sweetly soft
and leave a puddle

it didn't take much
the patterns had her in pieces /
her life, the stability of a game of jenga
not a question of if she'd fall
but when

now she's solid, concrete /
light a fire on her surface and
all she will do is blacken /
she can't be touched underneath

i love her this consistency /
peering under eyelids
i study her color and shape /
aching to to look more like the
predator
and less like the prey

// the tenacity of the women around me //

each blank space
is a chance

a chance to
feel unabashedly /
or to document
where you left your fingertips /
or to prove
that there's at least
one part about you
that's independent
of the root
from which we all
grow

// you are art //

there is more life:
purple blossoms contouring
oceans of green

what was mourned over and
thought to be lost
appears wet and weathered /
demanding to be brought
fresh
and with a heartbeat
back to the memory

this is spring /
soft urgency:
now is the time to grow

// season of change //

dispersed in the yucca and ocotillo, below the towering, sandy mountains and saguaro, i found myself in a dried up stream: amidst rocks sobered by long-gone rushing water, settled and sun-bleached sand, and suspicions of gila monsters somewhere nearby.

yet, more distracting than all this was a storm of butterflies: purple and white and small, filling my hair and getting caught between my knees. they would sweep and steam in the desert sun, coursing fleetingly and hurried. i lifted my arms up from my sides, as one does when they experience miraculous scenes, my palms instinctively and submissively turned up, willing, pining, to be lifted off the earth.

with childlike surprise, that butterfly rain turned into a butterfly river, thin and almost stagnant parts of the river bed held shallow dregs painted by the green of the old water and the purple of butterfly bodies, as thick in the water as they were in the air.

in distress, i saved one as it drowned and placed its light body on the sand. but in synchrony, another floated down and submitted to the waters' soft hands. i let go of my self-annointed role of interfering, sitting back on my haunches to witness death and life rolling around the desert air.

// life exists because of the dance she is in with death //

it immobilized me /
bloated me /
i swelled
so full of tears
waiting their turn
and emotions too dense
to sift through
with my fingers
or write about

when time and people
piled around me
the questions
on their tongues
poked holes
through my surface /
and although the pin-pricks hurt
the words dammed in
trickled out
leaving room
in my body to
breath

i
can
breath

// speak //

like temperature testing toes
the days ripple out from the one
where we left town
chasing the sun, moon and a change of
altitude

fitful roads of mist and sliding tires
of burning rubber and steam
books tucked into spaces
and hands holding across the two feet

auspicious unpaved roads
through the throat of a mountain
it is on no map
no plan
aloof from the scream of
electronic dependency

authenticity
gurgles her name
from the beginnings of puddles
that evolve into rivers
        we push our heads under
        the surface and listen
the water tells us stories
about the meaning of home

// painting new landscapes //

a wet wet Wood
where a slow spring
takes its time on
sweet Grasses, pores exploding with green /
and Trees
      with bases like
      wide smiles /
      on whose arms Birds lull
      each other awake with
      their esoteric language
and Those Trees who
      surrendered back down to the place
      that began them /
      hushed by Bugs slurping up their veins
      and Moss cuddling around its shape /
      coaxing it to softly succumb
      how sickly sweet /
the way a dead Tree
is the start of all fascinations
for a future Ecosystem

// cyclic //

people have left my mind bruised
my body stripped and solitaire in the emergency
room /
yet, not everything has been taken from me

i can still write

i can conjure words into poems and bury them in
the backyard, or burn them one by one. i'll slip them
under the bed—sly and dusty. i can eat my words,
take them like a fat pill and wash them down with
coffee. i can keep them where they'd last expect, on
the counter labeled "tax receipts". or as a flower petal,
i can press them to the gyri and sulci of my brain.
look for them, i dare you, dissect me. i vow to never
forget the scenes i paint phonologically, and they vow
to always find their way back to me.

but i can still write.

i am closed and small
a bud not yet trusting the spring /
but the words have space to make their way
          no matter the season
to my page

// at the moment when i thought i had
nothing, i realized i had everything //

MEGAN LEICK was born and raised in Wisconsin. She was a closeted poet throughout her youth but began to share her fascination with writing as a young adult, first through anonymous napkin poems at coffee shops and expanding to reading at poetry slams. She has been published in a University of Wisconsin-Stevens Point student publication, *Wordplay*, in the Spring of 2019 and Fall of 2018. Her poetry is cyclic, as it discusses themes of interpersonal violence and impermanence while also dancing with thoughts on intimacy and transformation. Megan currently works as a speech language pathologist, and on the side, enjoys a variety of passions, including biking, reading, and practicing yoga.

www.ingramcontent.com/pod-product-compliance
Lightning Source LLC
Chambersburg PA
CBHW030510130626
46549CB00007B/2928